NATIONAL GEOGRAPHIC

Who Looks After Me?

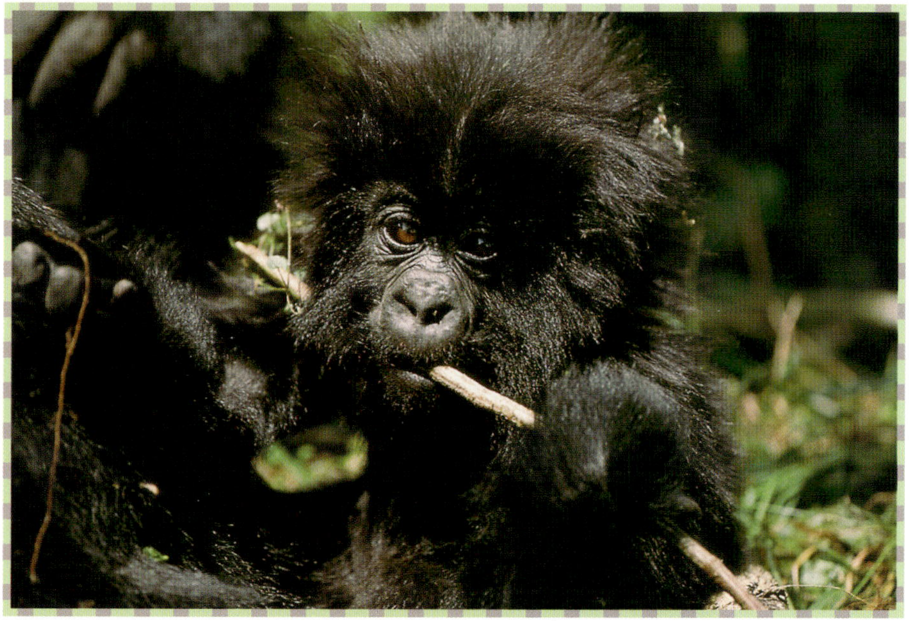

Dimi Stanos

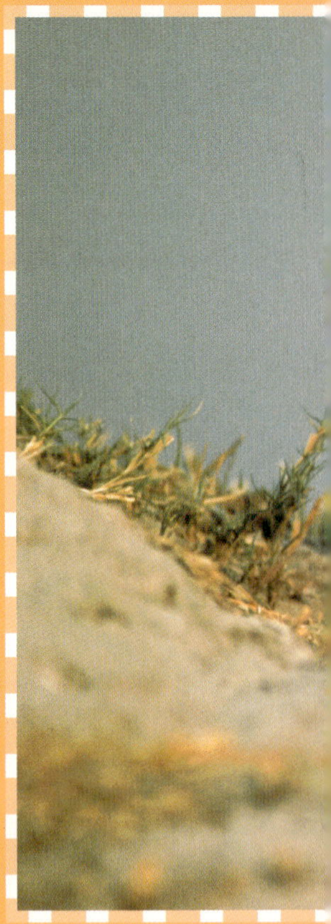

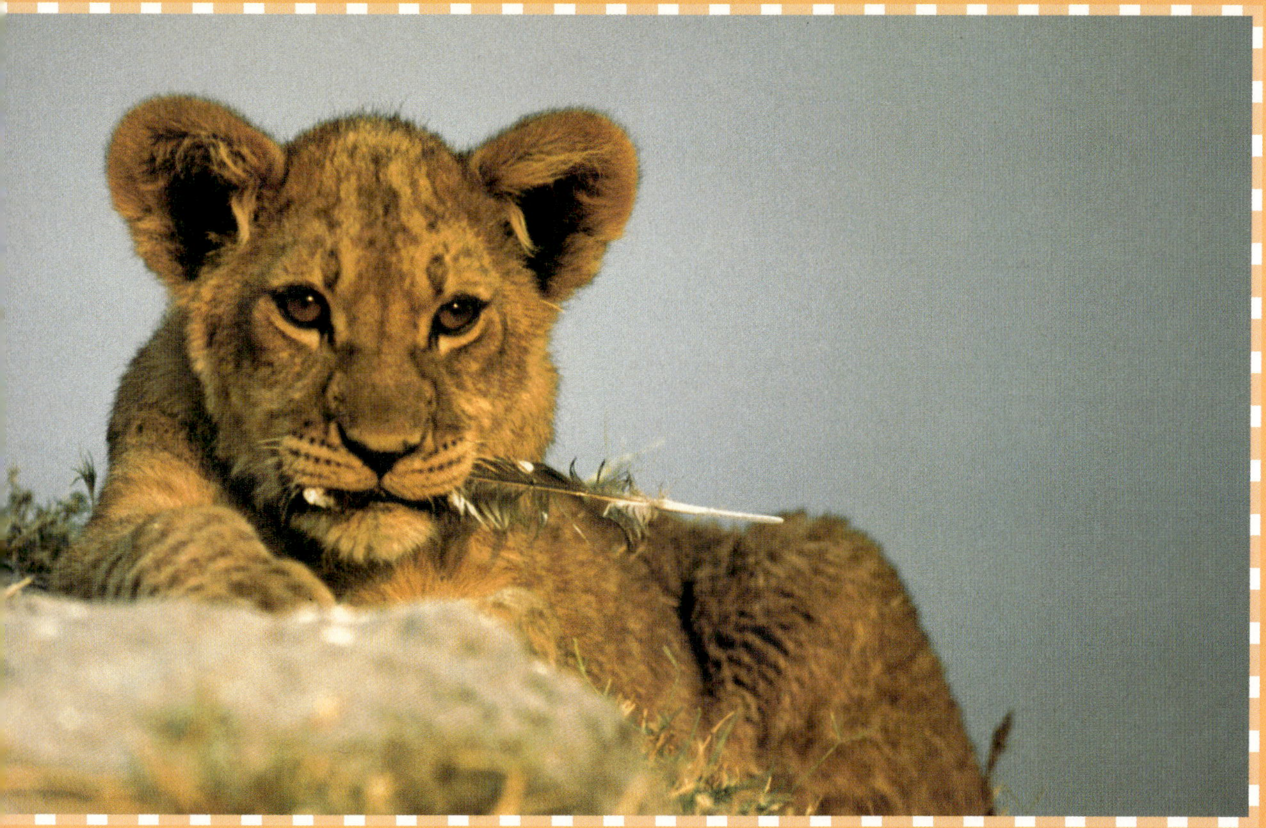

Who looks after me?

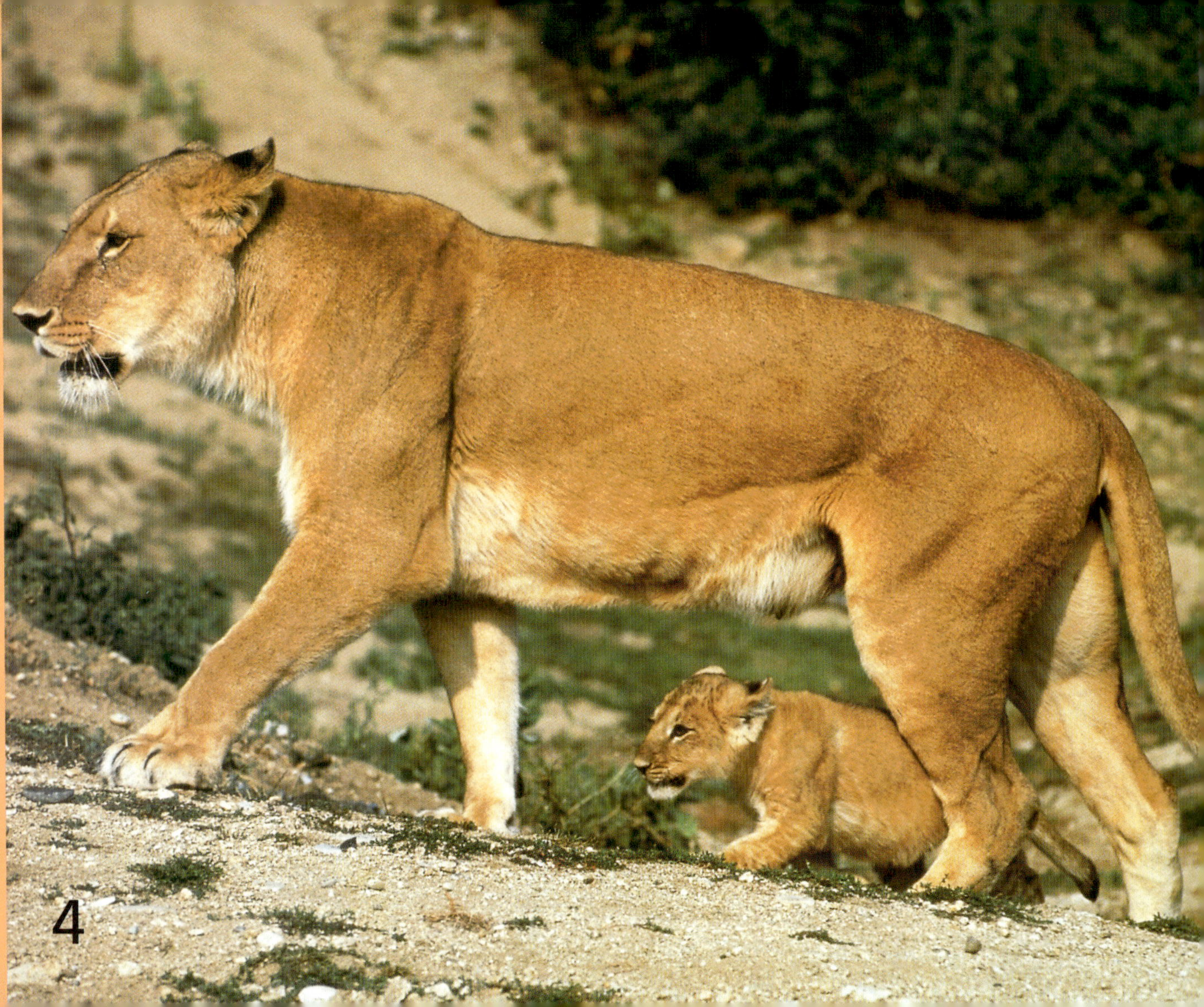

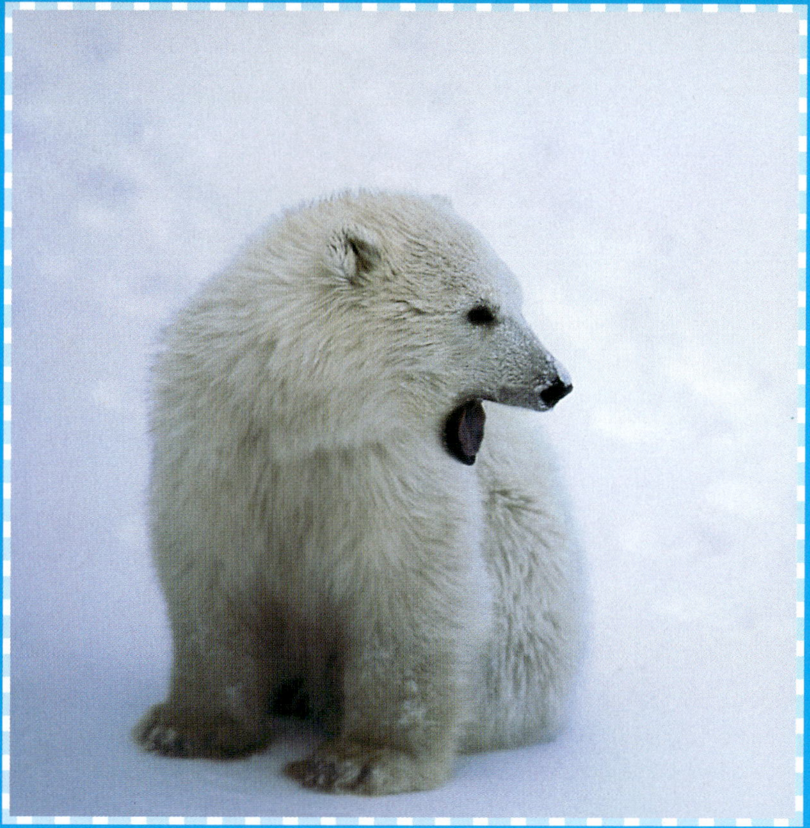

Who looks after me?

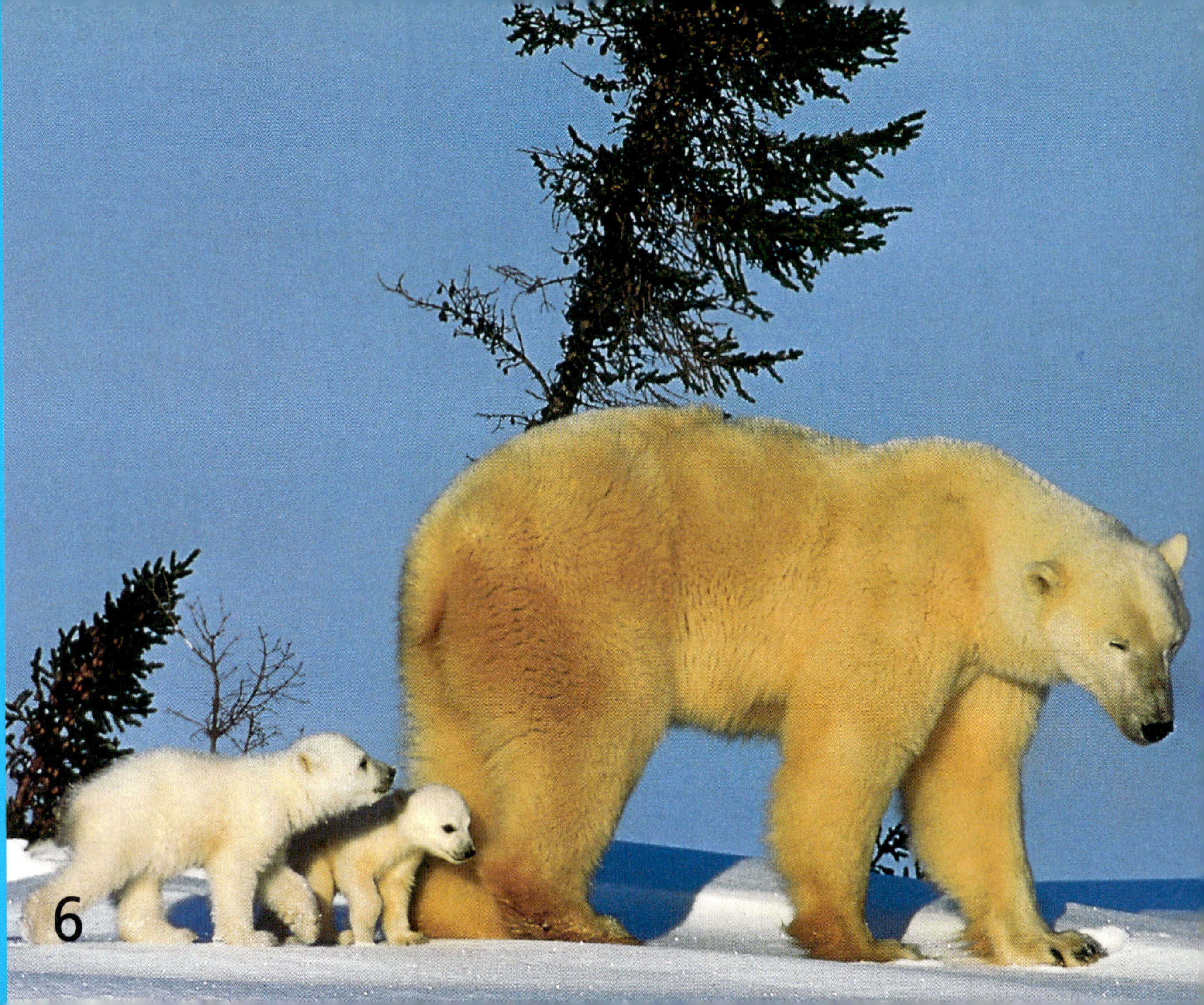

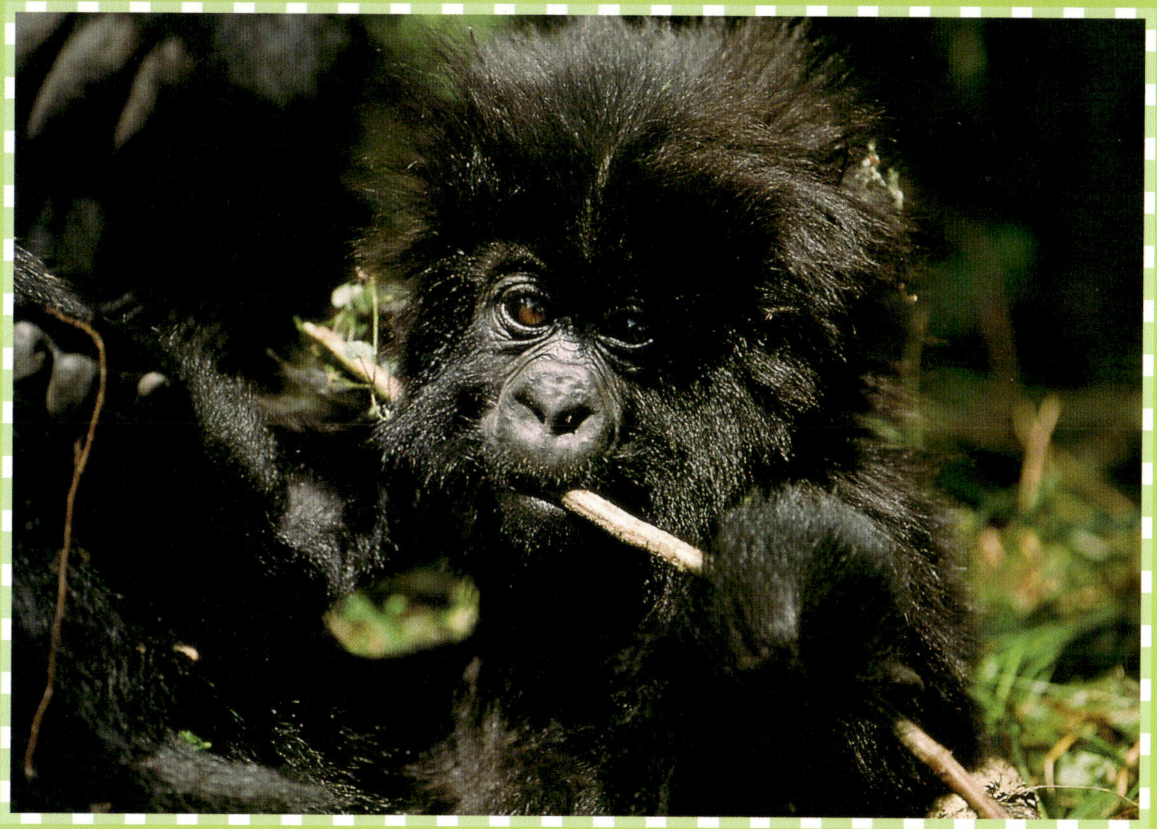

Who looks after me?

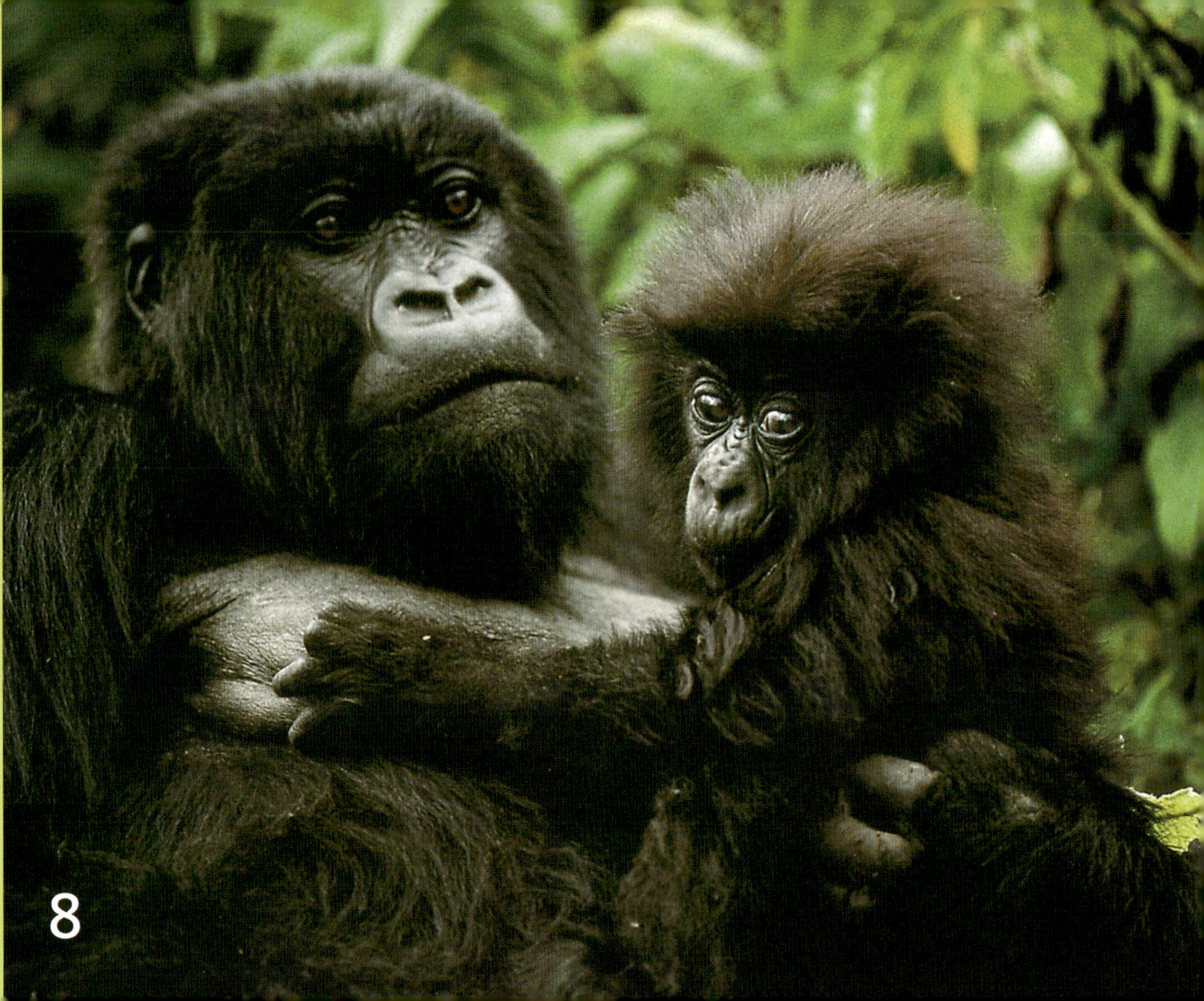

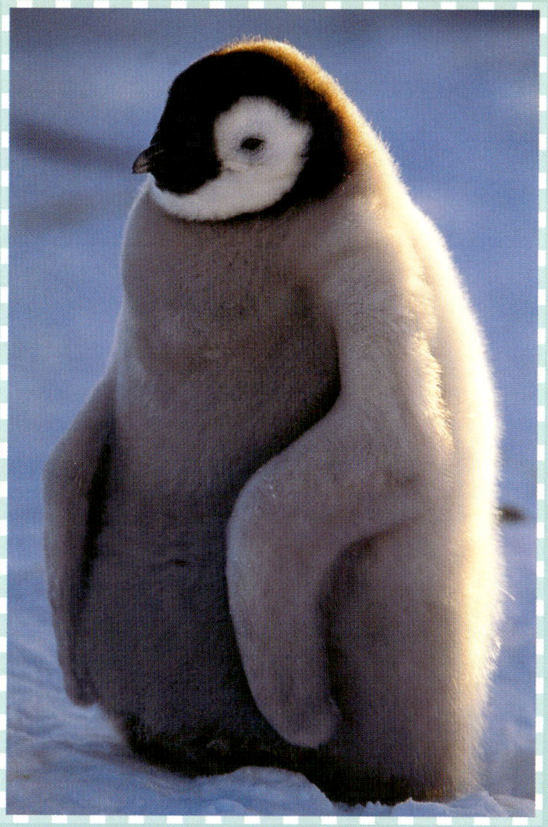

Who looks after me?

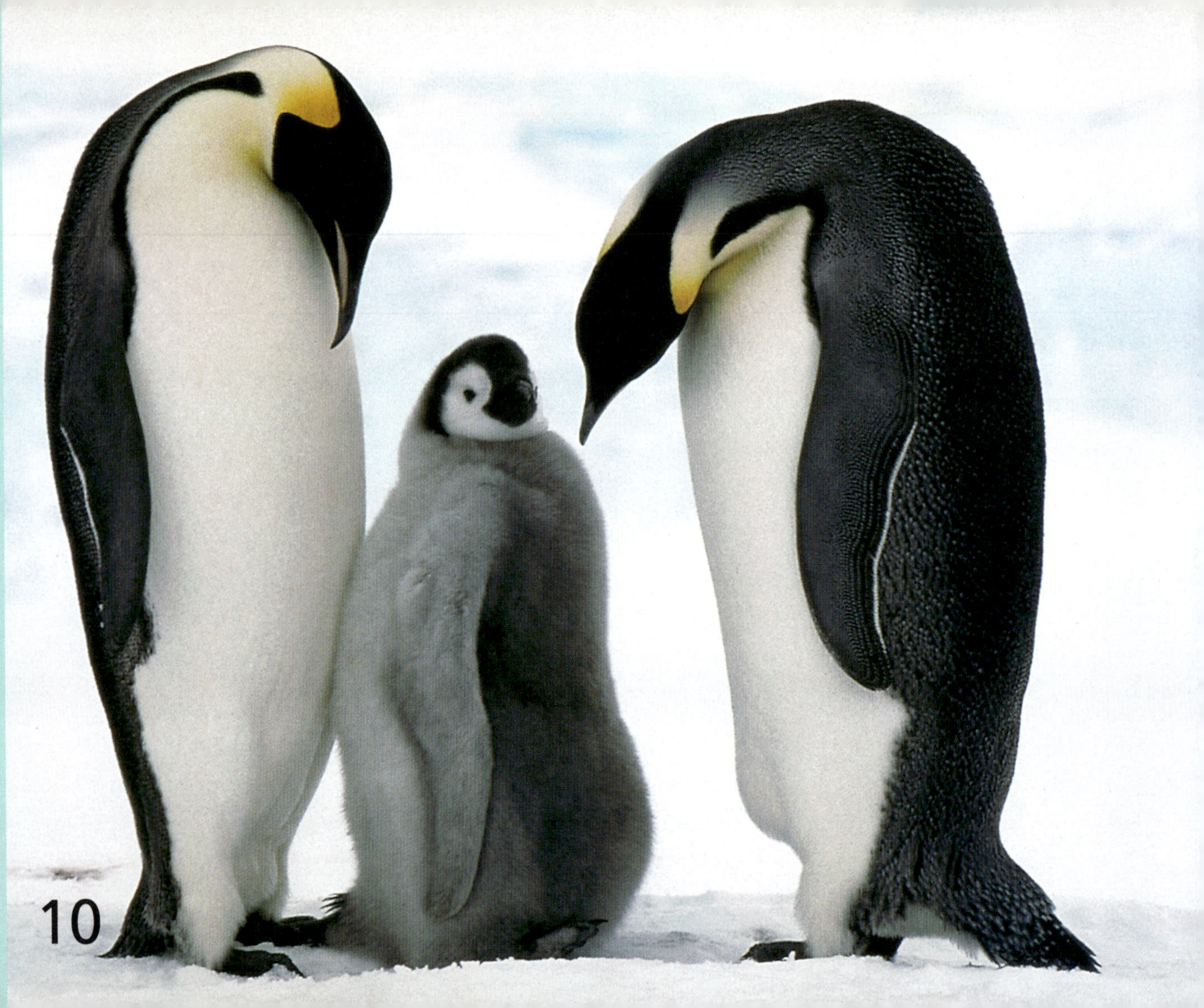

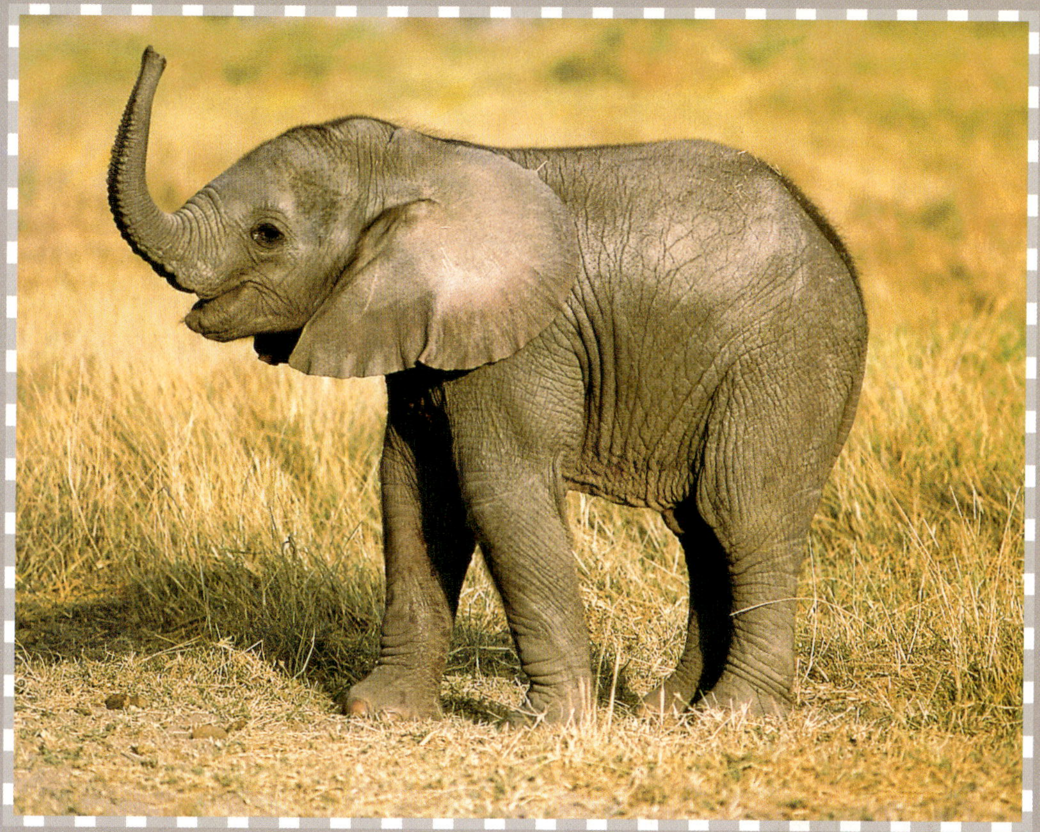

Who looks after me?

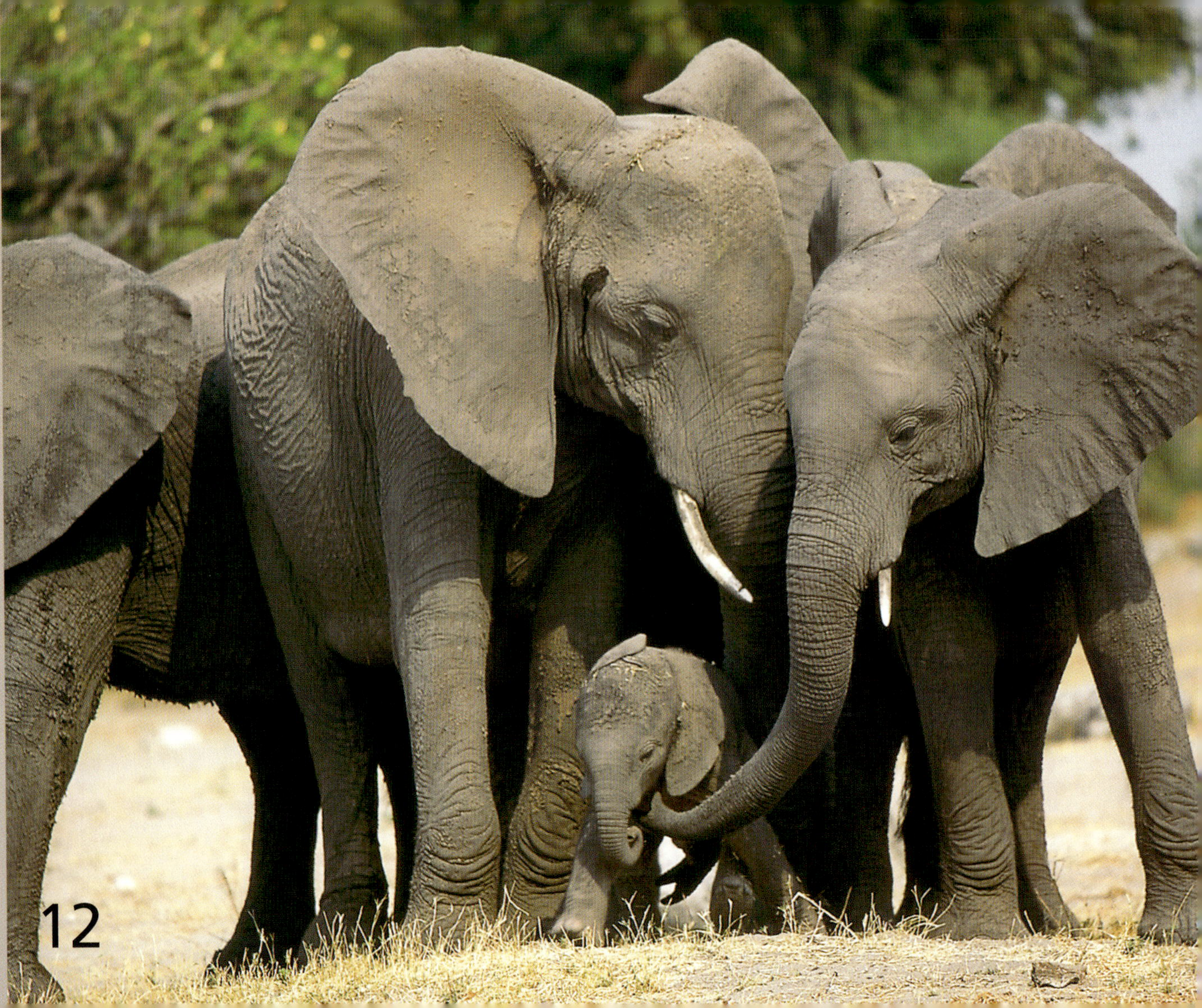